Puree Food Cookbook for Adults

The Essential Guide to Creating Delicious and Nutritious Easy Meals for People with Chewing, Swallowing Difficulties and Dysphagia

SALENA GREEN

Table of Contents

Introduction

When people think of pureed food, they often think of bland meals that are intended for infants or those who have difficulty swallowing. On the other hand, this perspective fails to take into account the many opportunities and unexpected advantages that it presents to individuals of all ages and abilities. Puree diets offer a multitude of benefits that go far beyond simply satisfying their basic nutritional requirements. Whether you are looking for novel approaches to incorporate more nutrients into your diet, exploring alternatives due to medical conditions such as dysphagia or dental issues, or simply a desire for softer textures, puree diets offer a wealth of advantages.

Benefits You Might Not Expect:

1. Improved Nutrition: The process of pureeing liberates the latent potential of a wide variety of substances. The tough vegetables, such as broccoli or kale, are transformed into a silky-smooth consistency, which makes them simpler to digest and absorb critical nutrients. Proteins such as chicken or fish may be blended into sauces that are rich in taste, guaranteeing that you will receive the advantages of these foods without having to worry about chewing them.

2. Dietary Inclusion: Pureed food provides an opportunity for people who have dysphagia, which is a condition that causes difficulty swallowing, as well as other medical disorders that impede chewing or digesting. It makes it possible for them to consume a greater range of meals and to keep up a diet that is both balanced and healthy, which is beneficial to their general health and well-being.

3. Creativity in the Kitchen: Never undervalue the potential of your culinary skills! Pureeing reveals a world of textures and taste combinations. Imagine silky smooth soups bursting with spices, creamy vegetable purees blended with herbs, or luscious fruit mousses for dessert. You may even adapt classic foods like lasagna or shepherd's pie into delectable, readily digestible pureed variants.

4. Easier Meal Planning: Pureeing streamlines meal preparation. With a blender or food processor, you can whip up healthful meals in minutes. Leftovers may be readily recycled, and pre-portioning pureed meals makes meal planning a snap, excellent for busy persons or those maintaining portion control.

5. Improved Digestion: Pureeing breaks down food into its most digestible form, placing less load on your digestive system. This may be especially good for persons with digestive difficulties or those recuperating from surgery.

6. Reduced Discomfort: For people with swallowing issues, pureeing food reduces the danger of choking and aspiration, enabling them to enjoy meals securely and pleasantly.

Getting Started with Puree Diets:

1. see Your Doctor: If you're contemplating a pureed diet for medical reasons, always see your doctor or a qualified dietitian first. They can examine your particular demands and propose the proper texture and consistency for your personal circumstances.

2. Explore the Options: Don't be intimidated! There's a plethora of knowledge and tools accessible online and in cookbooks devoted to pureed diets. Experiment with various recipes and ingredients to discover the textures and tastes you prefer.

3. Start Small: Incorporate pureed foods gradually into your diet. You may start with morning smoothies or snacks, then graduate to full meals as you learn what works best for you.

4. Embrace Flavor: Don't underestimate the power of spices and herbs! These may give depth and complexity to your pureed recipes, ensuring they're anything from boring.

5. Presentation Matters: Just because food is pureed doesn't mean it can't be visually pleasing. Use colorful garnishes, pour sauces, and arrange food imaginatively on your plate to make meals fun.

Tips, Techniques, Tools, and Recipe Adaption

Embarking on a puree diet doesn't imply compromising taste or culinary innovation. With the correct strategies, methods, equipment, and a flair for recipe modification, you can open a world of tasty and fulfilling pureed meals.

Pureeing Prowess: Tips & Techniques:

Start with Quality: Choose fresh, ripe ingredients for the best taste and texture. Overripe fruits and vegetables may blend differently, so try to discover your taste.

Cooking Matters: Depending on the desired consistency, simmer items until tender. Steaming or boiling maintains nutrients and textures better than frying.

Liquids are your Ally: Use broths, milk, cream, or even yogurt to modify the consistency and add flavor and moisture. Start with less liquid and add progressively until you achieve your desired texture.

Embrace Seasoning: Don't shy away from herbs, spices, and citrus — they are flavor powerhouses! Experiment with various combinations to create distinct profiles.

Batch it Up: Puree bigger amounts and freeze in portions for handy meals throughout the week. Remember to label and date for convenient usage.

Garnish like a Pro: A sprinkling of fresh herbs, roasted almonds, or a drop of sauce may improve even the simplest purée. Get creative and have fun!

Essential Equipment for Your Puree Pantry:

Immersion Blender: This flexible gadget works excellent for smaller amounts and directly in pots, making cleaning a joy.

Stand Blender: Powerful and efficient, great for big amounts and difficult ingredients.

Food Processor: Offers chopping and pureeing capabilities, suitable for materials with varying textures.

Fine-Mesh Sieve: For ultra-smooth textures, put strained purée through a sieve after mixing.

Tamper: Helps push viscous materials down towards the blades for uniform mixing.

Ice Cube Trays: Perfect for portioning and freezing individual servings.

Storage Containers: Choose air-tight containers to avoid freezer burn and keep freshness.

Adapting Recipes for Puree Perfection: Embrace Soups and Smoothies: Soups are inherently puree-friendly, while smoothies provide unlimited taste variations.

Think Soft and Moist: Look for meals containing soft cooked veggies, cooked meat, and creamy sauces.

Skip the Crunch: Avoid recipes using raw vegetables, nuts, and seeds, since they may not mix smoothly.

Adjust Cooking Times: Reduce cooking times somewhat, since blended components cook quicker.

Start Slowly and Blend Gradually: Add liquids progressively to reach the required consistency. Over-blending might make the purée gummy.

Get Creative with Substitutes: Replace solid items with their pureed equivalents. For example, use pureed sweet potato instead of mashed potatoes.

Don't Fear the Spices: Experiment with herbs and spices to compensate for texture loss and boost tastes.

Chapter 1: Breakfast

Pureed Banana Oatmeal

Prep Time: 5 minutes

Cooking Time: 10 minutes

Total Time: 15 minutes

Serving: 2

Ingredients:

- o *1 cup cooked oats*
- o *2 ripe bananas*

Directions:

1. Combine cooked oats with ripe bananas in a blender.
2. Blend until smooth consistency is reached.
3. Serve warm and enjoy!

Nutritional Value: (per serving)

- o Calories: 200
- o Protein: 5g
- o Fat: 2g
- o Carbohydrates: 45g
- o Fiber: 6g

Pureed Avocado Toast

Prep Time: 5 minutes

Cooking Time: N/A

Total Time: 5 minutes

Serving: 1

Ingredients:

- o *1 ripe avocado*
- o *1 teaspoon lemon juice*
- o *1 slice whole-grain toast*

Directions:

1. Scoop out the flesh of the ripe avocado into a blender.
2. Add lemon juice to the blender.
3. Blend until smooth.
4. Spread the pureed avocado mixture over the whole-grain toast.
5. Enjoy!

Nutritional Value: (per serving)

- o Calories: 220
- o Protein: 3g
- o Fat: 15g
- o Carbohydrates: 20g
- o Fiber: 8g

Pureed Berry Smoothie Bowl

Prep Time: 5 minutes

Cooking Time: N/A

Total Time: 5 minutes

Serving: 1

Ingredients:

- o *1 cup mixed berries (fresh or frozen)*
- o *1/2 cup yogurt*
- o *Splash of milk (as needed for desired consistency)*

Directions:

1. In a blender, combine mixed berries, yogurt, and a splash of milk.
2. Blend until smooth.
3. Pour the pureed berry mixture into a bowl.
4. Top with your favorite toppings like granola, nuts, or more berries.
5. Enjoy!

Nutritional Value: (per serving)

- o Calories: 180
- o Protein: 8g
- o Fat: 3g
- o Carbohydrates: 35g
- o Fiber: 8g

Pureed Sweet Potato Pancakes

Prep Time: 10 minutes

Cooking Time: 15 minutes

Total Time: 25 minutes

Serving: 4

Ingredients:

- 2 cups cooked sweet potatoes
- 1 cup pancake mix
- 1 egg
- 1/2 cup milk

Directions:

1. In a blender, combine cooked sweet potatoes, pancake mix, egg, and milk.
2. Blend until smooth.
3. Heat a lightly oiled skillet over medium heat.
4. Pour pancake batter onto the skillet.
5. Cook until bubbles appear on the surface, then turn and cook until golden brown.
6. Serve warm with your favorite toppings.

Nutritional Value: (per serving)

- o Calories: 250
- o Protein: 8g
- o Fat: 4g
- o Carbohydrates: 45g
- o Fiber: 5g

Pureed Spinach and Feta Omelets

Prep Time: 10 minutes

Cooking Time: 5 minutes

Total Time: 15 minutes

Serving: 1

Ingredients:

- o *2 cups cooked spinach*
- o *1/4 cup feta cheese*

- ○ *2 eggs*

Directions:

1. In a blender, combine cooked spinach, feta cheese, and eggs.
2. Blend until smooth.
3. Pour the mixture into a heated and greased skillet.
4. Cook until set, then fold and serve.
5. Enjoy your flavorful pureed omelet!

Nutritional Value: (per serving)

- ○ Calories: 280
- ○ Protein: 18g
- ○ Fat: 20g
- ○ Carbohydrates: 8g
- ○ Fiber: 4g

Pureed Mango Chia Pudding

Prep Time: 10 minutes

Cooking Time: N/A (Refrigerate for at least 4 hours or overnight)

Total Time: 4 hours 10 minutes

Serving: 2

Ingredients:

- o *2 ripe mangoes*
- o *1/4 cup chia seeds*
- o *1 cup almond milk*

Directions:

1. Blend ripe mangoes with almond milk until smooth.
2. Mix in chia seeds and refrigerate for at least 4 hours or overnight.
3. Stir before serving.
4. Enjoy the nutritious and tasty pureed mango chia pudding!

Nutritional Value: (per serving)

- o Calories: 220
- o Protein: 5g
- o Fat: 10g
- o Carbohydrates: 30g
- o Fiber: 10g

Pureed Pumpkin Porridge

Prep Time: 15 minutes

Cooking Time: 10 minutes

Total Time: 25 minutes

Serving: 2

Ingredients:

- o   *1 cup cooked pumpkin*
- o   *1/2 cup oats*
- o   *1/2 teaspoon cinnamon*
- o   *1/4 teaspoon nutmeg*

Directions:

1. Puree cooked pumpkin.
2. Cook oats according to package instructions.
3. Mix the pureed pumpkin into the cooked oats.
4. Add cinnamon and nutmeg, stir well.
5. Serve warm and enjoy your comforting pureed pumpkin porridge!

Nutritional Value: (per serving)

- o   Calories: 220
- o   Protein: 5g
- o   Fat: 2g
- o   Carbohydrates: 45g
- o   Fiber: 8g

Pureed Apple Cinnamon Quinoa

Prep Time: 10 minutes

Cooking Time: 15 minutes

Total Time: 25 minutes

Serving: 2

Ingredients:

- *1 cup cooked quinoa*
- *1/2 cup applesauce*
- *1 teaspoon cinnamon*

Directions:

1. Puree cooked quinoa with applesauce and cinnamon.
2. Heat the pureed mixture in a pan until warm.
3. Serve in bowls and sprinkle with additional cinnamon if desired.
4. Enjoy your hearty and nutritious pureed apple cinnamon quinoa!

Nutritional Value: (per serving)

- Calories: 250
- Protein: 8g
- Fat: 3g
- Carbohydrates: 50g
- Fiber: 6g

Pureed Carrot Ginger Soup

Prep Time: 15 minutes

Cooking Time: 25 minutes

Total Time: 40 minutes

Serving: 4

Ingredients:

- o *2 cups carrots, chopped*
- o *1 tablespoon fresh ginger, minced*
- o *1 onion, diced*
- o *4 cups vegetable broth*

Directions:

1. In a pot, cook carrots, ginger, and onion until softened.

2. Add vegetable broth and boil until veggies are soft.
3. Puree the soup until smooth.
4. Serve hot and enjoy this flavorful start to the day!

Nutritional Value: (per serving)

- o Calories: 120
- o Protein: 2g
- o Fat: 1g
- o Carbohydrates: 28g
- o Fiber: 5g

Pureed Greek Yogurt Parfait

Prep Time: 10 minutes

Cooking Time: N/A

Total Time: 10 minutes

Serving: 2

Ingredients:

- o *1 cup Greek yogurt*
- o *1 cup mixed fruits (berries, banana slices, etc.)*
- o *1/2 cup granola*

Directions:

1. Blend Greek yogurt until smooth.

2. In serving glasses, layer pureed yogurt with mixed fruits and granola.
3. Repeat layers as desired.
4. Enjoy this delicious and protein-packed breakfast parfait!

Nutritional Value: (per serving)

- o   Calories: 300
- o   Protein: 15g
- o   Fat: 8g
- o   Carbohydrates: 45g
- o   Fiber: 6g

Pureed Blueberry Almond Butter Toast

Prep Time: 5 minutes

Cooking Time: N/A

Total Time: 5 minutes

Serving: 1

Ingredients:

- o   *1/2 cup fresh blueberries*
- o   *2 tablespoons almond butter*
- o   *1 slice whole-grain toast*

Directions:

1. Blend fresh blueberries with almond butter until smooth.
2. Spread the pureed mixture on whole-grain toast.
3. Enjoy this nutrient-rich and flavorful breakfast option!

Nutritional Value: (per serving)

- o   Calories: 250
- o   Protein: 7g
- o   Fat: 12g
- o   Carbohydrates: 30g
- o   Fiber: 5g

Pureed Zucchini Frittata

Prep Time: 15 minutes

Cooking Time: 20 minutes

Total Time: 35 minutes

Serving: 4

Ingredients:

- o   *2 zucchinis, grated*
- o   *6 eggs*
- o   *1/2 cup shredded cheese (optional)*

Directions:

1. Preheat oven to 375°F (190°C).
2. Mix grated zucchini into beaten eggs.
3. Fill a greased ovenproof dish with the ingredients.
4. Bake the frittata until it sets and becomes a golden brown.
5. Slice and serve this unique and vegetable-packed morning meal!

Nutritional Value: (per serving)

o Calories: 180
o Protein: 12g
o Fat: 10g
o Carbohydrates: 8g
o Fiber: 2g

Pureed Cauliflower Breakfast Bowl

Prep Time: 10 minutes

Cooking Time: 15 minutes

Total Time: 25 minutes

Serving: 2

Ingredients:

- o *2 cups cooked cauliflower*
- o *1/2 teaspoon cumin*

- *1/4 teaspoon paprika*
- *Salt and pepper to taste*
- *2 poached eggs*
- *1 avocado, sliced*

Directions:

1. In a blender, combine cooked cauliflower, cumin, paprika, salt, and pepper.
2. Blend until smooth.
3. Divide the pureed cauliflower into bowls.
4. Top with poached eggs and sliced avocado.
5. Enjoy this savory and protein-packed pureed breakfast bowl!

Nutritional Value: (per serving)

- Calories: 300
- Protein: 15g
- Fat: 20g
- Carbohydrates: 20g | Fiber: 10g

Pureed Raspberry Chia Seed Pudding

Prep Time: 10 minutes

Cooking Time: N/A (Refrigerate for at least 4 hours or overnight)

Total Time: 4 hours 10 minutes

Serving: 2

Ingredients:

- o *1 cup raspberries*
- o *2 tablespoons chia seeds*
- o *1 cup coconut milk*

Directions:

1. Blend raspberries until smooth.
2. Mix in chia seeds and coconut milk, and refrigerate for at least 4 hours or overnight.
3. Stir before serving.
4. Enjoy this delightful and nutritious pureed raspberry chia seed pudding!

Nutritional Value: (per serving)

- o Calories: 220
- o Protein: 5g
- o Fat: 10g
- o Carbohydrates: 30g
- o Fiber: 10g

Pureed Broccoli and Cheese Oatmeal

Prep Time: 10 minutes

Cooking Time: 10 minutes

Total Time: 20 minutes

Serving: 2

Ingredients:

- o *1 cup cooked broccoli*
- o *1 cup rolled oats*
- o *1/2 cup shredded cheese*
- o *Salt and pepper to taste*

Directions:

1. Puree cooked broccoli in a blender.
2. Cook rolled oats according to package instructions.
3. Mix the pureed broccoli into the cooked oatmeal.
4. Add shredded cheese, salt, and pepper, and stir until the cheese is melted.
5. Serve warm and enjoy this savory and satisfying pureed breakfast option!

Nutritional Value: (per serving)

- o Calories: 300
- o Protein: 15g
- o Fat: 10g
- o Carbohydrates: 40g
- o Fiber: 8g

Chapter 2: Lunch

Pureed Butternut Squash Soup with a Touch of Nutmeg

Prep Time: 15 minutes

Cooking Time: 30 minutes

Total Time: 45 minutes

Serving: 4

Ingredients:

- o *1 medium butternut squash, peeled and chopped*
- o *1 onion, chopped*
- o *2 cloves garlic, minced*
- o *4 cups vegetable broth*
- o *1/2 teaspoon nutmeg*

Directions:

1. In a saucepan, sauté onions and garlic until softened.
2. Add chopped butternut squash and veggie broth. Simmer until the squash is soft.
3. Puree the soup until smooth, adding nutmeg while mixing.
4. Season with salt and pepper to taste.
5. Serve hot, served with a dusting of nutmeg.

Nutritional Value: (per serving)

- o Calories: 120
- o Protein: 2g
- o Fat: 1g
- o Carbohydrates: 28g
- o Fiber: 5g

Pureed Roasted Red Pepper and Tomato Bisque

Prep Time: 15 minutes

Cooking Time: 40 minutes

Total Time: 55 minutes

Serving: 4

Ingredients:

- o *3 red bell peppers, roasted and peeled*
- o *1 onion, chopped*
- o *2 cloves garlic, minced*
- o *1 can (28 oz) chopped tomatoes*
- o *4 cups vegetable broth*

Directions:

1. In a saucepan, sauté onions and garlic until softened.

2. Add roasted red peppers, diced tomatoes, and vegetable broth. Simmer for 30 minutes.
3. Puree the soup until smooth.
4. Season with salt and pepper to taste.
5. Serve hot, garnished with a drizzle of olive oil if preferred.

Nutritional Value: (per serving)

- o Calories: 150
- o Protein: 3g
- o Fat: 2g
- o Carbohydrates: 30g
- o Fiber: 7g

Pureed Cauliflower and Leek Soup with a Hint of Thyme

Prep Time: 15 minutes

Cooking Time: 25 minutes

Total Time: 40 minutes

Serving: 4

Ingredients:

- o *1 head cauliflower, chopped*
- o *2 leeks, sliced*
- o *2 cloves garlic, minced*
- o *4 cups vegetable broth*
- o *1 teaspoon thyme*

Directions:

1. In a saucepan, sauté leeks and garlic until softened.
2. Add chopped cauliflower and vegetable broth. Simmer until cauliflower is soft.
3. Puree the soup until smooth, adding thyme while mixing.
4. Season with salt and pepper to taste.
5. Serve hot, garnished with a sprinkling of thyme.

Nutritional Value: (per serving)

- Calories: 90
- Protein: 3g
- Fat: 1g
- Carbohydrates: 20g
- Fiber: 5g

Pureed Broccoli and Cheddar Cheese Soup

Prep Time: 15 minutes

Cooking Time: 25 minutes

Total Time: 40 minutes

Serving: 4

Ingredients:

- *2 cups broccoli florets*
- *1 onion, chopped*

- o *2 cloves garlic, minced*
- o *4 cups vegetable broth*
- o *1 cup shredded cheddar cheese*

Directions:

1. In a saucepan, sauté onions and garlic until softened.
2. Add broccoli and vegetable broth. Simmer until broccoli is tender.
3. Puree the soup until smooth, then whisk in cheddar cheese until melted.
4. Season with salt and pepper to taste.
5. Serve hot, garnished with more cheese if desired.

Nutritional Value: (per serving)

- o Calories: 180
- o Protein: 8g
- o Fat: 10g
- o Carbohydrates: 15g
- o Fiber: 4g

Pureed Carrot and Ginger Bisque

Prep Time: 15 minutes

Cooking Time: 25 minutes

Total Time: 40 minutes

Serving: 4

Ingredients:

- o *2 cups carrots, chopped*
- o *one tablespoon fresh ginger, minced one onion, diced*
- o *4 cups vegetable broth*
- o *Salt and pepper to taste*

Directions:

1. In a saucepan, sauté onions and ginger until mellow.
2. Add diced carrots and vegetable broth. Simmer until carrots are soft.
3. Puree the soup until smooth.
4. Season with salt and pepper to taste.
5. Serve hot, topped with a drizzle of olive oil or a sprinkling of fresh herbs.

Nutritional Value: (per serving)

o Calories: 120
o Protein: 2g
o Fat: 1g
o Carbohydrates: 28g
o Fiber: 5g

Pureed Spinach and Feta Quiche

Prep Time: 15 minutes

Cooking Time: 40 minutes

Total Time: 55 minutes

Serving: 6

Ingredients:

- o *2 cups fresh spinach*
- o *1/2 cup feta cheese, crumbled*

- o *6 eggs*
- o *1 cup milk*
- o *Salt and pepper to taste*

Directions:

1. Preheat the oven to 375°F (190°C).
2. In a blender, add fresh spinach, feta cheese, eggs, and milk. Blend until smooth.
3. Pour the mixture into a greased pie plate.
4. Bake for 40 minutes or until the quiche is set and golden brown.
5. Allow it to cool somewhat before slicing and serving.

Nutritional Value: (per serving)

- o Calories: 180
- o Protein: 12g
- o Fat: 10g
- o Carbohydrates: 10g
- o Fiber: 2g

Pureed Sweet Potato and Black Bean Soup

Prep Time: 20 minutes

Cooking Time: 30 minutes

Total Time: 50 minutes

Serving: 4

Ingredients:

- o *2 cups sweet potatoes, peeled and diced*

- o *One can (15 ounce) black beans, drained and rinsed*
- o *1 onion, chopped 2 cloves garlic, minced*
- o *4 cups vegetable broth*
- o *1 teaspoon cumin*

Directions:

1. In a saucepan, sauté onions and garlic until softened.
2. Add chopped sweet potatoes, black beans, cumin, and vegetable broth. Simmer until sweet potatoes are soft.
3. Puree the soup until smooth.
4. To taste, add more salt, pepper, and cumin.
5. Serve hot, topped with a dollop of Greek yogurt or a sprinkling of fresh cilantro.

Nutritional Value: (per serving)

- o Calories: 220
- o Protein: 8g
- o Fat: 1g
- o Carbohydrates: 45g
- o Fiber: 8g

Pureed Pea and Mint Soup

Prep Time: 15 minutes

Cooking Time: 20 minutes

Total Time: 35 minutes

Serving: 4

Ingredients:

- o *2 cups peas (fresh or frozen)*
- o *1 onion, diced*
- o *2 cups vegetable broth*
- o *1/4 cup fresh mint leaves*
- o *Salt and pepper to taste*

Directions:

1. In a saucepan, sauté onions until tender.
2. Add peas, vegetable broth, and fresh mint. Simmer until peas are soft.
3. Puree the soup until smooth.
4. Season with salt and pepper to taste.
5. Serve hot, garnished with more mint leaves or a swirl of yogurt.

Nutritional Value: (per serving)

- o Calories: 150
- o Protein: 7g
- o Fat: 1g
- o Carbohydrates: 30g
- o Fiber: 8g

Pureed Zucchini and Basil Gazpacho

Prep Time: 15 minutes

Cooking Time: 0 minutes (No cooking needed)

Total Time: 15 minutes

Serving: 4

Ingredients:

- o *4 medium zucchinis, chopped*
- o *1 cup fresh basil leaves*
- o *2 cloves garlic, minced*
- o *2 tablespoons olive oil*
- o *2 teaspoons white wine vinegar*
- o *Salt and pepper to taste*

Directions:

1. In a blender, mix chopped zucchini, basil, garlic, olive oil, and white wine vinegar.
2. Blend until smooth.
3. Season with salt and pepper to taste.
4. Chill in the refrigerator before serving.
5. Serve chilled, garnished with more basil leaves or a drizzle of olive oil.

Nutritional Value: (per serving)

- o Calories: 120
- o Protein: 3g
- o Fat: 8g
- o Carbohydrates: 12g
- o Fiber: 4g

Pureed Lentil and Vegetable Curry

Prep Time: 15 minutes

Cooking Time: 30 minutes

Total Time: 45 minutes

Serving: 4

Ingredients:

- o *1 cup dry lentils, washed and drained*
- o *1 onion, chopped*
- o *2 carrots, diced*

- o *2 tomatoes, chopped*
- o *2 cloves garlic, minced*
- o *1 tablespoon curry powder*
- o *4 cups vegetable broth*

Directions:

1. In a saucepan, sauté onions and garlic until softened.
2. Add lentils, carrots, tomatoes, curry powder, and vegetable broth. Simmer until lentils are soft.
3. Puree the soup until smooth.
4. Season with salt and pepper to taste.
5. Serve hot, topped with a dollop of yogurt and chopped cilantro.

Nutritional Value: (per serving)

- o Calories: 250
- o Protein: 15g
- o Fat: 2g
- o Carbohydrates: 45g
- o Fiber: 15g

Pureed Asparagus with Potato Chowder

Prep Time: 20 minutes

Cooking Time: 25 minutes

Total Time: 45 minutes

Serving: 4

Ingredients:

- *1 bunch asparagus, trimmed and chopped*
- *2 potatoes, peeled and diced*
- *1 onion, diced*
- *2 cloves garlic, minced*
- *4 cups vegetable broth*
- *1/2 cup heavy cream (optional)*

Directions:

1. In a saucepan, sauté onions and garlic until softened.
2. Add asparagus, potatoes, and vegetable broth. Simmer until veggies are soft.
3. Puree the soup until smooth.
4. Stir in heavy cream if desired.
5. Season with salt and pepper to taste.
6. Serve hot, served with a sprinkling of chives or grated cheese.

Nutritional Value: (per serving)

- Calories: 200
- Protein: 5g
- Fat: 8g
- Carbohydrates: 30g
- Fiber: 6g

Pureed Mushroom and Wild Rice Soup

Prep Time: 15 minutes

Cooking Time: 40 minutes

Total Time: 55 minutes

Serving: 4

Ingredients:

- o *2 cups mushrooms, sliced*
- o *1 cup wild rice, cooked*
- o *1 onion, chopped*
- o *2 cloves garlic, minced*
- o *4 cups vegetable broth*
- o *1/2 cup heavy cream (optional)*

Directions:

1. In a saucepan, sauté onions and garlic until softened.
2. Add mushrooms, cooked wild rice, and vegetable broth. Simmer until mushrooms are soft.
3. Puree the soup until smooth.
4. Stir in heavy cream if desired.
5. Season with salt and pepper to taste.
6. Serve hot, garnished with a sprinkling of fresh parsley or thyme.

Nutritional Value: (per serving)

- Calories: 250
- Protein: 8g
- Fat: 10g
- Carbohydrates: 35g
- Fiber: 5g

Pureed Chickpea and Tahini Hummus:

Prep Time: 10 minutes

Cooking Time: 0 minutes (No cooking needed)

Total Time: 10 minutes

Serving: 8

Ingredients:

- *One can (15 ounce) chickpeas, drained and rinsed*
- *1/4 cup tahini*
- *2 cloves garlic, minced*
- *2 tablespoons olive oil*
- *2 teaspoons lemon juice*
- *Salt and cumin to taste*

Directions:

1. In a food processor, blend chickpeas, tahini, garlic, olive oil, and lemon juice.
2. Puree until smooth, adding water if required for desired consistency.

3. Season with salt and cumin to taste.
4. Serve chilled, topped with a drizzle of olive oil and a sprinkle of paprika.

Nutritional Value: (per serving - 2 teaspoons)

- o Calories: 70
- o Protein: 2g
- o Fat: 5g
- o Carbohydrates: 5g
- o Fiber: 2g

Pureed Avocado and Lime Gazpacho

Prep Time: 15 minutes

Cooking Time: 0 minutes (No cooking needed)

Total Time: 15 minutes

Serving: 4

Ingredients:

- o *2 ripe avocados, peeled and pitted*
- o *1 cucumber, peeled and cut*
- o *1/4 cup fresh cilantro*
- o *1/4 cup red onion, chopped*
- o *2 limes, juiced*
- o *2 cups vegetable broth*
- o *Salt and pepper to taste*

Directions:

1. In a blender, mix avocados, cucumber, cilantro, red onion, lime juice, and vegetable broth.
2. Puree till smooth.
3. Season with salt and pepper to taste.
4. Chill in the refrigerator before serving.
5. Serve cool, garnished with extra cilantro and a lime wedge.

Nutritional Value: (per serving)

o Calories: 180
o Protein: 2g
o Fat: 15g
o Carbohydrates: 12g
o Fiber: 7g

Pureed Roast Chicken and Vegetable Stew

Prep Time: 20 minutes

Cooking Time: 45 minutes

Total Time: 1 hour 5 minutes

Serving: 6

Ingredients:

- o *2 cups roast chicken, shredded*
- o *1 onion, chopped*
- o *2 carrots, diced*

- ○ *2 potatoes, peeled and diced*
- ○ *2 cloves garlic, minced*
- ○ *4 cups chicken broth*
- ○ *1/2 cup peas (fresh or frozen)*

Directions:

1. In a saucepan, sauté onions and garlic until softened.
2. Add shredded roast chicken, carrots, potatoes, and chicken broth. Simmer until veggies are soft.
3. Puree the stew till smooth, retaining some pieces as desired.
4. Stir in peas and simmer until cooked through.
5. Season with salt and pepper to taste.
6. Serve hot, garnished with fresh herbs like parsley or thyme.

Nutritional Value: (per serving)

- ○ Calories: 280
- ○ Protein: 20g
- ○ Fat: 8g
- ○ Carbohydrates: 30g
- ○ Fiber: 5g

Chapter 3: Dinner

Pureed Butternut Squash and Sage Risotto

Prep Time: 15 minutes

Cooking Time: 30 minutes

Total Time: 45 minutes

Serving: 4

Ingredients:

- o *1 cup Arborio rice*
- o *2 cups butternut squash, peeled and diced*
- o *1 onion, diced*

- o *4 cups vegetable broth, heated*
- o *1/4 cup fresh sage leaves, chopped*
- o *1/2 cup Parmesan cheese, grated*
- o *Salt and pepper to taste*

Directions:

1. In a pan, sauté onions until translucent.
2. Add Arborio rice and cook until lightly toasted.
3. Gradually add hot vegetable broth, stirring continuously until absorbed.
4. Stir in diced butternut squash and continue adding broth until rice is creamy and cooked.
5. Puree the risotto with fresh sage leaves and Parmesan cheese until smooth.
6. Season with salt and pepper to taste.
7. Serve hot, garnished with additional sage leaves and a sprinkle of Parmesan.

Nutritional Value: (per serving)

- o Calories: 350
- o Protein: 8g
- o Fat: 6g
- o Carbohydrates: 70g
- o Fiber: 5g

Pureed Roasted Garlic and Cauliflower Mashed Potatoes

Prep Time: 15 minutes

Cooking Time: 30 minutes

Total Time: 45 minutes

Serving: 6

Ingredients:

- *1 head cauliflower, cut into florets*

- o *4 cloves garlic, roasted*
- o *4 cups potatoes, peeled and diced*
- o *1/2 cup milk*
- o *2 tablespoons butter*
- o *Salt and pepper to taste*

Directions:

1. Steam cauliflower and potatoes until tender.
2. In a blender, puree cauliflower, roasted garlic, milk, and butter until smooth.
3. Mash potatoes and fold in the cauliflower puree until well combined.
4. Season with salt and pepper to taste.
5. Serve hot, garnished with chopped chives or parsley.

Nutritional Value: (per serving)

- o Calories: 180
- o Protein: 4g
- o Fat: 5g
- o Carbohydrates: 30g
- o Fiber: 5g

Pureed Spinach and Artichoke Stuffed Chicken Breast

Prep Time: 20 minutes

Cooking Time: 30 minutes

Total Time: 50 minutes

Serving: 4

Ingredients:

- o *4 boneless, skinless chicken breasts*
- o *1 cup spinach, wilted and chopped*
- o *1/2 cup artichoke hearts, chopped*
- o *1/4 cup cream cheese*
- o *1/4 cup Parmesan cheese, grated*
- o *Salt and pepper to taste*

Directions:

1. Preheat oven to 375°F (190°C).
2. In a bowl, mix chopped spinach, artichoke hearts, cream cheese, and Parmesan.
3. Cut a pocket into each chicken breast and stuff with the spinach and artichoke mixture.
4. Bake until chicken is cooked through.
5. Puree any remaining spinach and artichoke mixture until smooth.
6. Serve hot, drizzled with the pureed sauce.

Nutritional Value: (per serving)

- o Calories: 280
- o Protein: 35g
- o Fat: 12g
- o Carbohydrates: 5g

- Fiber: 2g

Pureed Sweet Potato and Coconut Curry

Prep Time: 20 minutes

Cooking Time: 30 minutes

Total Time: 50 minutes

Serving: 4

Ingredients:

- *2 large sweet potatoes, peeled and diced*
- *1 onion, diced*
- *2 cloves garlic, minced*
- *1 can (14 oz) coconut milk*

- ○ *2 tablespoons curry powder*
- ○ *1 tablespoon coconut oil*
- ○ *Salt and pepper to taste*

Directions:

1. In a pot, sauté onions and garlic in coconut oil until softened.
2. Add sweet potatoes, coconut milk, and curry powder. Simmer until sweet potatoes are tender.
3. Puree the curry until smooth.
4. Season with salt and pepper to taste.
5. Serve hot, garnished with a swirl of coconut milk and chopped cilantro.

Nutritional Value: (per serving)

- ○ Calories: 300
- ○ Protein: 4g
- ○ Fat: 15g
- ○ Carbohydrates: 40g
- ○ Fiber: 6g

Pureed Roasted Red Pepper and Tomato Pasta Sauce

Prep Time: 15 minutes

Cooking Time: 30 minutes

Total Time: 45 minutes

Serving: 4

Ingredients:

- o *2 red bell peppers, roasted and peeled*
- o *4 tomatoes, diced*
- o *1 onion, chopped*
- o *2 cloves garlic, minced*
- o *2 tablespoons olive oil*
- o *1 teaspoon dried basil*
- o *Salt and pepper to taste*

Directions:

1. In a pan, sauté onions and garlic in olive oil until softened.
2. Add diced tomatoes and roasted red peppers. Simmer until tomatoes are soft.
3. Puree the sauce until smooth.
4. Season with dried basil, salt, and pepper to taste.
5. Serve over cooked pasta, garnished with fresh basil and grated Parmesan.

Nutritional Value: (per serving)

- o Calories: 120
- o Protein: 2g
- o Fat: 7g
- o Carbohydrates: 15g | Fiber: 4g

Pureed Broccoli and Cheddar Stuffed Bell Peppers

Prep Time: 20 minutes

Cooking Time: 30 minutes

Total Time: 50 minutes

Serving: 4

Ingredients:

- o *4 bell peppers, halved and seeds removed*
- o *2 cups broccoli florets, steamed*
- o *1 cup cheddar cheese, shredded*
- o *1 onion, diced*

- o *2 cloves garlic, minced*
- o *1 cup cooked quinoa*

Directions:

1. Preheat oven to 375°F (190°C).
2. In a bowl, mix steamed broccoli, cheddar cheese, diced onion, minced garlic, and cooked quinoa.
3. Puree the mixture until smooth.
4. Stuff bell peppers with the pureed mixture.
5. Bake until peppers are tender and filling is heated through.
6. Serve hot, garnished with chopped parsley or green onions.

Nutritional Value: (per serving)

- o Calories: 250
- o Protein: 12g
- o Fat: 10g
- o Carbohydrates: 30g
- o Fiber: 6g

Pureed Carrot and Ginger-Glazed Salmon

Prep Time: 15 minutes

Cooking Time: 15 minutes

Total Time: 30 minutes

Serving: 4

Ingredients:

- o *4 salmon fillets*
- o *1 cup carrots, grated*
- o *2 tablespoons ginger, minced*
- o *1/4 cup soy sauce*
- o *2 tablespoons honey*
- o *2 cloves garlic, minced*

Directions:

1. In a bowl, mix grated carrots, minced ginger, soy sauce, honey, and minced garlic.
2. Puree the glaze until smooth.
3. Brush the salmon fillets with the pureed glaze.
4. Bake or grill salmon until cooked through.
5. Serve hot, drizzled with additional glaze and garnished with sesame seeds.

Nutritional Value: (per serving)

- o Calories: 300
- o Protein: 25g
- o Fat: 12g
- o Carbohydrates: 20g
- o Fiber: 2g

Pureed Zucchini and Basil Pesto Pasta

Prep Time: 15 minutes

Cooking Time: 10 minutes

Total Time: 25 minutes

Serving: 4

Ingredients:

- o *2 zucchinis, spiralized or thinly sliced*
- o *1 cup fresh basil leaves*
- o *1/2 cup pine nuts*
- o *1/2 cup Parmesan cheese, grated*
- o *1/2 cup olive oil*
- o *2 cloves garlic, minced*

Directions:

1. In a blender, combine zucchini, fresh basil, pine nuts, grated Parmesan, olive oil, and minced garlic.
2. Puree until the pesto is smooth.
3. Toss the zucchini and basil pesto with cooked pasta.
4. Serve warm, garnished with additional Parmesan and a sprinkle of pine nuts.

Nutritional Value: (per serving)

- o Calories: 350

- o Protein: 8g
- o Fat: 30g
- o Carbohydrates: 15g
- o Fiber: 3g

Pureed Mushroom and Thyme-Infused Lentil Stew

Prep Time: 15 minutes

Cooking Time: 45 minutes

Total Time: 1 hour

Serving: 4

Ingredients:

- o 1 cup green or brown lentils, rinsed
- o 2 cups mushrooms, sliced
- o 1 onion, chopped
- o 2 cloves garlic, minced
- o 4 cups vegetable broth
- o 1 teaspoon thyme leaves
- o Salt and pepper to taste

Directions:

1. In a pot, sauté onions and garlic until softened.
2. Add mushrooms, lentils, thyme, and vegetable broth. Simmer until lentils are tender.
3. Puree the stew until smooth.

4. Season with salt and pepper to taste.
5. Serve hot, garnished with a sprinkle of fresh thyme.

Nutritional Value: (per serving)

- o   Calories: 250
- o   Protein: 15g
- o   Fat: 2g
- o   Carbohydrates: 45g
- o   Fiber: 12g

Pureed Asparagus and Parmesan Risotto

Prep Time: 20 minutes

Cooking Time: 30 minutes

Total Time: 50 minutes

Serving: 4

Ingredients:

- o   *1 cup Arborio rice*
- o   *1 bunch asparagus, trimmed and chopped*
- o   *1 onion, diced*
- o   *4 cups vegetable broth, heated*
- o   *1/2 cup Parmesan cheese, grated*
- o   *2 tablespoons olive oil*
- o   *Salt and pepper to taste*

Directions:

1. In a pan, sauté onions in olive oil until translucent.
2. Add Arborio rice and cook until lightly toasted.
3. Gradually add hot vegetable broth, stirring continuously until absorbed.
4. Stir in chopped asparagus and continue adding broth until rice is creamy and cooked.
5. Puree the risotto with Parmesan cheese until smooth.
6. Season with salt and pepper to taste.
7. Serve hot, garnished with additional Parmesan and a drizzle of olive oil.

Nutritional Value: (per serving)

- Calories: 350
- Protein: 10g
- Fat: 8g
- Carbohydrates: 60g
- Fiber: 5g

Pureed Cauliflower and Leek Gratin

Prep Time: 20 minutes

Cooking Time: 40 minutes

Total Time: 1 hour

Serving: 6

Ingredients:

- o *1 head cauliflower, cut into florets*
- o *2 leeks, sliced*
- o *2 cups milk*

- o *1/2 cup Gruyere cheese, grated*
- o *2 tablespoons butter*
- o *2 tablespoons flour*
- o *Salt and nutmeg to taste*

Directions:

1. Steam cauliflower until tender.
2. In a pan, sauté leeks in butter until softened. Add flour and cook briefly.
3. Gradually whisk in milk to create a sauce. Stir in Gruyere cheese until melted.
4. Puree cauliflower and leek mixture until smooth.
5. Season with salt and nutmeg to taste.
6. Transfer to a baking dish and bake until golden brown.
7. Serve hot, garnished with fresh herbs.

Nutritional Value: (per serving)

- o Calories: 200
- o Protein: 8g
- o Fat: 12g
- o Carbohydrates: 15g
- o Fiber: 4g

Pureed Eggplant and Chickpea Curry

Prep Time: 15 minutes

Cooking Time: 30 minutes

Total Time: 45 minutes

Serving: 4

Ingredients:

- o *1 large eggplant, diced*
- o *1 can (15 oz) chickpeas, drained and rinsed*
- o *1 onion, chopped*
- o *2 tomatoes, diced*
- o *2 cloves garlic, minced*
- o *1/4 cup curry powder*
- o *1 cup coconut milk*
- o *2 tablespoons olive oil*
- o *Salt and cilantro to taste*

Directions:

1. In a pan, sauté onions and garlic in olive oil until softened.
2. Add diced eggplant, chickpeas, tomatoes, curry powder, and coconut milk. Simmer until eggplant is tender.
3. Puree the curry until smooth.
4. Season with salt and garnish with cilantro.
5. Serve hot, over rice or with naan bread.

Nutritional Value: (per serving)

- o Calories: 300
- o Protein: 10g
- o Fat: 15g
- o Carbohydrates: 40g
- o Fiber: 12g

Pureed Pumpkin and Sage-Infused Quinoa

Prep Time: 15 minutes

Cooking Time: 20 minutes

Total Time: 35 minutes

Serving: 4

Ingredients:

- o *1 cup quinoa, rinsed*
- o *2 cups pumpkin, peeled and diced*
- o *1 onion, chopped*
- o *2 cloves garlic, minced*
- o *4 cups vegetable broth*
- o *1 tablespoon fresh sage leaves, chopped*
- o *2 tablespoons olive oil*
- o *Salt and pepper to taste*

Directions:

1. In a pot, sauté onions and garlic in olive oil until softened.
2. Add diced pumpkin, quinoa, fresh sage, and vegetable broth. Simmer until quinoa is cooked.
3. Puree the mixture until smooth.
4. Season with salt and pepper to taste.
5. Serve hot, garnished with a drizzle of olive oil and additional sage.

Nutritional Value: (per serving)

o Calories: 280
o Protein: 8g
o Fat: 8g
o Carbohydrates: 45g
o Fiber: 6g

Pureed Beet and Goat Cheese Risotto

Prep Time: 20 minutes

Cooking Time: 30 minutes

Total Time: 50 minutes

Serving: 4

Ingredients:

- *1 cup Arborio rice*
- *2 beets, roasted and diced*

- *1 onion, diced*
- *4 cups vegetable broth, heated*
- *1/2 cup goat cheese, crumbled*
- *2 tablespoons olive oil*
- *Salt and pepper to taste*

Directions:

1. In a pan, sauté onions in olive oil until translucent.
2. Add Arborio rice and cook until lightly toasted.
3. Gradually add hot vegetable broth, stirring continuously until absorbed.
4. Stir in roasted beets and continue adding broth until rice is creamy and cooked.
5. Puree the risotto with crumbled goat cheese until smooth.
6. Season with salt and pepper to taste.
7. Serve hot, garnished with additional goat cheese and a sprinkle of fresh herbs.

Nutritional Value: (per serving)

- Calories: 320
- Protein: 8g
- Fat: 10g
- Carbohydrates: 50g
- Fiber: 4g

Pureed Kale and White Bean Soup with Smoked Paprika

Prep Time: 15 minutes

Cooking Time: 30 minutes

Total Time: 45 minutes

Serving: 6

Ingredients:

- *1 bunch kale, stemmed and chopped*
- *2 cans (15 oz each) white beans, drained and rinsed*
- *1 onion, chopped*
- *2 carrots, diced*
- *2 cloves garlic, minced*
- *4 cups vegetable broth*
- *1 teaspoon smoked paprika*
- *2 tablespoons olive oil*
- *Salt and pepper to taste*

Directions:

1. In a pot, sauté onions and garlic in olive oil until softened.
2. Add chopped kale, diced carrots, white beans, smoked paprika, and vegetable broth. Simmer until vegetables are tender.
3. Puree the soup until smooth.

4. Season with salt and pepper to taste.
5. Serve hot, garnished with a drizzle of olive oil and a pinch of smoked paprika.

Nutritional Value: (per serving)

- Calories: 220
- Protein: 10g
- Fat: 5g
- Carbohydrates: 35g
- Fiber: 10g

Chapter 4: Snacks & Sides

Flavorful Dips & Hummus: Pureed Roasted Red Pepper and Walnut Dip

Prep Time: 15 minutes

Cooking Time: 10 minutes

Total Time: 25 minutes

Serving: 8

Ingredients:

- o *2 red bell peppers, roasted and peeled*
- o *1 cup walnuts, toasted 2 cloves garlic, minced*
- o *2 tablespoons olive oil*
- o *1 tablespoon lemon juice*
- o *Salt and pepper to taste*

Directions:

1. In a food processor, mix roasted red peppers, toasted walnuts, chopped garlic, olive oil, and lemon juice.
2. Puree until smooth, adding additional olive oil if required.
3. Season with salt and pepper to taste.

4. Serve chilled, topped with chopped parsley and extra walnuts.

Nutritional Value: (per serving - 2 teaspoons)

- o Calories: 120
- o Protein: 3g
- o Fat: 11g
- o Carbohydrates: 4g
- o Fiber: 1g

White Bean and Rosemary Hummus

Prep Time: 10 minutes

Cooking Time: 0 minutes (No cooking needed)

Total Time: 10 minutes

Serving: 8

Ingredients:

- o *one can (15 ounce) white beans, drained and rinsed*
- o *2 tablespoons tahini*
- o *1 clove garlic, minced*
- o *2 tablespoons fresh rosemary, chopped*
- o *2 tablespoons olive oil*
- o *Juice of 1 lemon*
- o *Salt and pepper to taste*

Directions:

1. In a food processor, combine white beans, tahini, minced garlic, chopped rosemary, olive oil, and lemon juice.
2. Puree until smooth, adding additional olive oil if required.
3. Season with salt and pepper to taste.
4. Serve chilled, drizzled with additional olive oil, and topped with fresh rosemary.

Nutritional Value: (per serving - 2 teaspoons)

o Calories: 90
o Protein: 3g
o Fat: 4g
o Carbohydrates: 10g
o Fiber: 3g

Pureed Black Bean and Avocado Dip

Prep Time: 10 minutes

Cooking Time: 0 minutes (No cooking needed)

Total Time: 10 minutes

Serving: 8

Ingredients:

- one can (15 ounce) black beans, drained and rinsed
- 2 ripe avocados, peeled and pitted 1 lime, juiced 2 cloves garlic, minced 1/4 cup cilantro, chopped
- Salt and cumin to taste

Directions:

1. In a food processor, blend black beans, avocados, lime juice, minced garlic, and cilantro.
2. Puree till smooth.
3. Season with salt and cumin to taste.
4. Serve chilled, topped with extra cilantro and a lime wedge.

Nutritional Value: (per serving - 2 teaspoons)

- Calories: 80
- Protein: 3g
- Fat: 5g
- Carbohydrates: 8g
- Fiber: 4g

Spinach with Feta Yogurt Dip

Prep Time: 15 minutes

Cooking Time: 0 minutes (No cooking needed)

Total Time: 15 minutes

Serving: 8

Ingredients:

- o *1 cup spinach, wilted and chopped*
- o *1/2 cup feta cheese, crumbled*
- o *1 cup Greek yogurt*
- o *2 tablespoons olive oil*
- o *1 clove garlic, minced*
- o *Salt and pepper to taste*

Directions:

1. In a bowl, add wilted and chopped spinach, crumbled feta, Greek yogurt, olive oil, and minced garlic.
2. Mix until completely blended.
3. Season with salt and pepper to taste.
4. Serve chilled, topped with a drizzle of olive oil and more feta.

Nutritional Value: (per serving - 2 teaspoons)

- o Calories: 70
- o Protein: 4g
- o Fat: 5g
- o Carbohydrates: 3g
- o Fiber: 1g

Pureed Cauliflower with Garlic Mashed Potatoes

Prep Time: 15 minutes

Cooking Time: 20 minutes

Total Time: 35 minutes

Serving: 6

Ingredients:

- o 1 head cauliflower, cut into florets
- o 4 big potatoes, peeled and chopped
- o 4 cloves garlic, minced
- o 1/2 cup milk
- o 2 tablespoons butter
- o Salt and pepper to taste

Directions:

1. Steam cauliflower and potatoes till tender.
2. In a blender, combine cauliflower, diced potatoes, minced garlic, milk, and butter until smooth.
3. Season with salt and pepper to taste.
4. Garnish with chopped parsley or chives and serve hot.

Nutritional Value: (per serving)

- o Calories: 150
- o Protein: 4g
- o Fat: 3g
- o Carbohydrates: 30g
- o Fiber: 5g

Creamy Spinach and Artichoke Puree

Prep Time: 10 minutes

Cooking Time: 10 minutes

Total Time: 20 minutes

Serving: 4

Ingredients:

- o *2 cups fresh spinach, wilted and chopped*
- o *1 can (14 oz) artichoke hearts, drained*
- o *1/2 cup cream cheese*
- o *1/4 cup grated Parmesan cheese*
- o *1 clove garlic, minced*
- o *Salt and pepper to taste*

Directions:

1. In a blender, purée wilted spinach, drained artichoke hearts, cream cheese, Parmesan cheese, and minced garlic until smooth.
2. Season with salt and pepper to taste.

3. Serve warm, topped with more Parmesan and a sprinkling of paprika.

Nutritional Value: (per serving)

- o Calories: 180
- o Protein: 6g
- o Fat: 12g
- o Carbohydrates: 10g
- o Fiber: 4g

Pureed Sweet Potato and Cinnamon Mash

Prep Time: 15 minutes

Cooking Time: 25 minutes

Total Time: 40 minutes

Serving: 4

Ingredients:

- o *2 big sweet potatoes, peeled and chopped*
- o *1/4 cup milk*
- o *2 tablespoons butter*
- o *1 teaspoon ground cinnamon*
- o *1 tablespoon maple syrup (optional)*
- o *Salt to taste*

Directions:

1. Boil or simmer sweet potatoes until fork-tender.

2. In a blender, mix sweet potatoes, milk, butter, ground cinnamon, and maple syrup until smooth.
3. Season with salt to taste.
4. Serve warm, drizzled with extra maple syrup if desired.

Nutritional Value: (per serving)

o Calories: 160
o Protein: 2g
o Fat: 5g
o Carbohydrates: 30g
o Fiber: 4g

Silky Carrot and Ginger Puree

Prep Time: 10 minutes

Cooking Time: 15 minutes

Total Time: 25 minutes

Serving: 4

Ingredients:

o *4 cups carrots, peeled and sliced*
o *1 tablespoon fresh ginger, grated*
o *1/2 cup vegetable broth*
o *2 tablespoons olive oil*
o *Salt and pepper to taste*

Directions:

1. Steam or boil carrots until soft.
2. In a blender, mix cooked carrots, grated ginger, vegetable broth, and olive oil until smooth.
3. Season with salt and pepper to taste.
4. Serve hot, garnished with a drizzle of olive oil and fresh parsley.

Nutritional Value: (per serving)

o   Calories: 120
o   Protein: 1g
o   Fat: 7g
o   Carbohydrates: 15g
o   Fiber: 4g

Spreads & Toppings for Crackers & Bread:

Pureed Olive Tapenade with Sundried Tomatoes

Prep Time: 15 minutes

Cooking Time: 0 minutes (No cooking needed)

Total Time: 15 minutes

Serving: 8

Ingredients:

- o *1 cup black olives, pitted*
- o *1/2 cup Kalamata olives, pitted*
- o *1/4 cup sundried tomatoes, drained*
- o *2 cloves garlic, minced*
- o *2 tablespoons capers*
- o *2 tablespoons olive oil*
- o *Fresh parsley for garnish*

Directions:

1. In a food processor, blend black olives, Kalamata olives, sundried tomatoes, chopped garlic, capers, and olive oil.
2. Puree till smooth.
3. Serve chilled, garnished with fresh parsley.

Nutritional Value: (per serving - 2 teaspoons)

- o Calories: 80
- o Protein: 1g
- o Fat: 7g
- o Carbohydrates: 4g
- o Fiber: 2g

Whipped Feta and Roasted Pepper Spread

Prep Time: 10 minutes

Cooking Time: 0 minutes (No cooking needed)

Total Time: 10 minutes

Serving: 8

Ingredients:

- o *1 cup feta cheese, crumbled*
- o *1/2 cup roasted red peppers, drained and diced*
- o *2 tablespoons Greek yogurt*
- o *1 tablespoon olive oil*
- o *Fresh basil for garnish*

Directions:

1. In a blender, mix feta cheese, roasted red peppers, Greek yogurt, and olive oil.
2. Blend until the mixture becomes smooth and creamy.
3. Serve cold, garnished with fresh basil.

Nutritional Value: (per serving - 2 tablespoons)

- o Calories: 70
- o Protein: 3g
- o Fat: 5g
- o Carbohydrates: 3g
- o Fiber: 1g

Roasted Eggplant with Tahini Spread

Prep Time: 15 minutes

Cooking Time: 20 minutes

Total Time: 35 minutes

Serving: 8

Ingredients:

- o *1 big eggplant, cut*
- o *2 tablespoons tahini*
- o *2 cloves garlic, minced*
- o *2 teaspoons lemon juice*
- o *2 tablespoons olive oil*
- o *Salt and pepper to taste*

Directions:

1. Roast eggplant slices till tender.
2. In a food processor, mix roasted eggplant, tahini, minced garlic, lemon juice, and olive oil.
3. Puree till smooth.
4. Season with salt and pepper to taste.
5. Serve refrigerated or at room temperature.

Nutritional Value: (per serving - 2 teaspoons)

- o Calories: 60
- o Protein: 1g
- o Fat: 5g

- o Carbohydrates: 4g
- o Fiber: 2g

Avocado and Lime Cream Cheese Spread

Prep Time: 10 minutes

Cooking Time: 0 minutes (No cooking needed)

Total Time: 10 minutes

Serving: 8

Ingredients:

- o *1 ripe avocado, peeled and pitted*
- o *4 ounces cream cheese, softened*
- o *1 lime, juiced Zest of 1 lime*
- o *Salt and pepper to taste*

Directions:

1. In a bowl, mash the ripe avocado.
2. Add softened cream cheese, lime juice, and lime zest. Mix until completely blended.
3. Season with salt and pepper to taste.
4. Serve cold, as a spread or dip.

Nutritional Value: (per serving - 2 teaspoons)

- o Calories: 80
- o Protein: 1g

- Fat: 7g
- Carbohydrates: 3g
- Fiber: 2g

Healthy Sweet Treats:

Pureed Mango and Coconut Chia Pudding

Prep Time: 10 minutes

Cooking Time: 0 minutes (No cooking needed)

Total Time: 4 hours (Chilling time)

Serving: 4

Ingredients:

- *1 cup ripe mango, diced*
- *1 can (14 oz) coconut milk*
- *1/4 cup chia seeds*
- *1 tablespoon honey or maple syrup (optional)*

Directions:

1. In a blender, purée ripe mango until smooth.
2. In a dish, blend mango puree, coconut milk, chia seeds, and honey (if using).

3. Refrigerate for at least 4 hours or overnight, enabling chia seeds to swell and form a pudding-like consistency.
4. Serve chilled, topped with more mango slices or coconut flakes.

Nutritional Value: (per serving)

- o Calories: 220
- o Protein: 3g
- o Fat: 18g
- o Carbohydrates: 15g
- o Fiber: 7g

Smooth Vanilla and Banana Yogurt Parfait

Prep Time: 10 minutes

Cooking Time: 0 minutes (No cooking needed)

Total Time: 10 minutes

Serving: 2

Ingredients:

- o *1 cup Greek yogurt*
- o *1 teaspoon vanilla extract*
- o *1 banana, sliced*
- o *2 tablespoons granola*
- o *Honey for drizzling (optional)*

Directions:

1. In a dish, combine Greek yogurt with vanilla extract.
2. In serving glasses, add the vanilla yogurt, banana slices, and granola.
3. Layers should be added until the glass is full.
4. Drizzle with honey if preferred.
5. Serve immediately.

Nutritional Value: (per serving)

- Calories: 250
- Protein: 15g
- Fat: 8g
- Carbohydrates: 30g
- Fiber: 4g

Silken Chocolate with Almond Butter Mousse

Prep Time: 15 minutes

Cooking Time: 0 minutes (No cooking needed)

Total Time: 2 hours (Chilling time)

Serving: 4

Ingredients:

- *1 cup silken tofu*

- o *1/4 cup almond butter*
- o *1/4 cup cocoa powder*
- o *3 tablespoons maple syrup or agave nectar*
- o *1 teaspoon vanilla extract*

Directions:

1. In a blender, mix silken tofu, almond butter, chocolate powder, maple syrup, and vanilla extract.
2. Blend until smooth and creamy.
3. Place in the fridge to chill for a minimum of two hours.
4. Serve chilled, topped with shaved chocolate or chopped almonds.

Nutritional Value: (per serving)

- o Calories: 180
- o Protein: 8g
- o Fat: 12g
- o Carbohydrates: 15g
- o Fiber: 3g

Pureed Mixed Berry and Yogurt Ice Pops

Prep Time: 10 minutes

Freezing Time: 4 hours

Total Time: 4 hours and 10 minutes

Serving: 6 popsicles

Ingredients:

- o *two cups mixed berries (strawberries, blueberries, raspberries)*
- o *1 cup Greek yogurt*
- o *2 tablespoons honey*
- o *1 teaspoon lemon juice*

Directions:

1. In a blender, purée mixed berries, Greek yogurt, honey, and lemon juice until smooth.
2. Pour the mixture into popsicle molds.
3. Place the popsicle sticks in and freeze until solid, about 4 hours.
4. Run molds under warm water to release popsicles before serving.

Nutritional Value: (per popsicle)

- o Calories: 60
- o Protein: 3g
- o Fat: 1g
- o Carbohydrates: 12g
- o Fiber: 2g

Coconut and Pineapple Smoothie Popsicles

Prep Time: 10 minutes

Freezing Time: 4 hours

Total Time: 4 hours and 10 minutes

Serving: 6 popsicles

Ingredients:

- o *1 cup coconut milk*
- o *1 cup pineapple chunks*
- o *1 banana*
- o *2 tablespoons shredded coconut (optional)*
- o *1 tablespoon honey or agave nectar*

Directions:

1. In a blender, combine coconut milk, pineapple chunks, banana, shredded coconut (if using), and honey until smooth.
2. Pour the mixture into popsicle molds.
3. Place the popsicle sticks in and freeze until solid, about 4 hours.
4. Run molds under warm water to release popsicles before serving.

Nutritional Value: (per popsicle)

- o Calories: 90
- o Protein: 1g

- o Fat: 4g
- o Carbohydrates: 15g
- o Fiber: 2g

Pureed Watermelon and Mint Granita

Prep Time: 10 minutes

Freezing Time: 4 hours

Total Time: 4 hours and 10 minutes

Serving: 4

Ingredients:

- o *4 cups seedless watermelon, cubed*
- o *2 tablespoons fresh mint leaves, chopped*
- o *2 tablespoons lime juice*
- o *2 tablespoons honey*

Directions:

1. In a blender, mix watermelon, mint leaves, lime juice, and honey until smooth.
2. Pour the mixture into a shallow dish and set it in the freezer.
3. Every 30 minutes, scrape the mixture with a fork to produce a granita texture.
4. Continue freezing and scraping until thoroughly frozen.

5. Serve in chilled dishes, topped with fresh mint.

Nutritional Value: (per serving)

- o Calories: 60
- o Protein: 1g
- o Fat: 0g
- o Carbohydrates: 16g
- o Fiber: 1g

Mango and Kiwi Sorbet Swirl

Prep Time: 15 minutes

Freezing Time: 4 hours

Total Time: 4 hours and 15 minutes

Serving: 4

Ingredients:

- o *2 ripe mangoes, peeled and diced*
- o *4 kiwis, peeled and sliced*
- o *2 tablespoons honey or agave nectar*
- o *1 tablespoon lime juice*

Directions:

1. In a blender, mix chopped mangoes with honey and lime juice until smooth.

2. In a separate blender, purée sliced kiwis until smooth.
3. Layer mango and kiwi purees in popsicle molds, producing a swirl appearance.
4. Place the popsicle sticks in and freeze until solid, about 4 hours.
5. Run molds under warm water to release popsicles before serving.

Nutritional Value: (per popsicle)

o Calories: 70 Protein: 1g
o Fat: 0g
o Carbohydrates: 18g
o Fiber: 3g

Chapter 5: Desserts & Drinks

Puddings & Mousses:
Silken Chocolate and Hazelnut Mousse:

Prep Time: 15 minutes

Cooking Time: 0 minutes (No cooking needed)

Total Time: 2 hours (Chilling time)

Serving: 4

Ingredients:

- o   *1 cup silken tofu*
- o   *1/4 cup hazelnut spread*
- o   *1/4 cup cocoa powder*
- o   *3 tablespoons maple syrup or agave nectar*

Directions:

1. In a blender, mix silken tofu, hazelnut spread, chocolate powder, and maple syrup.
2. Blend until smooth and creamy.
3. Place in the fridge to chill for a minimum of two hours.
4. Serve chilled, topped with chopped hazelnuts or shaved chocolate.

Nutritional Value: (per serving)

- o Calories: 160
- o Protein: 4g
- o Fat: 8g
- o Carbohydrates: 20g
- o Fiber: 3g

Vanilla Bean with Raspberry Chia Seed Pudding

Prep Time: 10 minutes

Chilling Time: 4 hours or overnight

Total Time: 4 hours and 10 minutes

Serving: 4

Ingredients:

- o *1 cup almond milk*
- o *1/4 cup chia seeds*
- o *1 vanilla bean, scraped (or 1 teaspoon vanilla essence)*
- o *1 cup fresh raspberries*
- o *2 tablespoons maple syrup*

Directions:

1. In a dish, combine almond milk, chia seeds, scraped vanilla bean (or vanilla essence), and maple syrup.
2. Let it rest in the refrigerator for at least 4 hours or overnight, enabling the chia seeds to absorb the liquid and develop a pudding-like consistency.
3. Before serving, top the chia pudding with fresh raspberries.
4. Serve cold.

Nutritional Value: (per serving)

o Calories: 120
o Protein: 3g
o Fat: 6g
o Carbohydrates: 15g
o Fiber: 7g

Espresso-Infused Tiramisu Parfait

Prep Time: 20 minutes

Chilling Time: 4 hours or overnight

Total Time: 4 hours and 20 minutes

Serving: 4

Ingredients:

o *1 cup strong brewed espresso, chilled*

- *1/2 cup mascarpone cheese*
- *1/4 cup sugar*
- *1 teaspoon vanilla extract*
- *Ladyfinger cookies*
- *Cocoa powder for dusting*

Directions:

1. In a bowl, mix together mascarpone cheese, sugar, and vanilla extract until smooth.
2. In serving glasses, arrange ladyfinger biscuits coated in espresso and mascarpone mixture.
3. Repeat the layers, concluding with a layer of mascarpone mixture on top.
4. Dust with chocolate powder.
5. Place in the fridge to chill for a minimum of four hours or overnight.
6. Serve cold.

Nutritional Value: (per serving)

- Calories: 300
- Protein: 5g
- Fat: 18g
- Carbohydrates: 30g
- Fiber: 1g

Coconut with Mango Tapioca Pudding

Prep Time: 15 minutes

Cooking Time: 20 minutes

Total Time: 35 minutes

Serving: 4

Ingredients:

- o *1/2 cup tiny pearl tapioca*
- o *2 cups coconut milk*
- o *1/4 cup sugar*
- o *1 ripe mango, diced*
- o *Toasted coconut flakes for garnish*

Directions:

1. In a saucepan, soak tapioca in coconut milk for 30 minutes.
2. Add sugar to the pot and simmer over medium heat until tapioca pearls are transparent.
3. Cool the tapioca pudding and refrigerate until cool.
4. Before serving, top the tapioca pudding with chopped mango.
5. Garnish with toasted coconut flakes.
6. Serve cold.

Nutritional Value: (per serving)

- Calories: 250
- Protein: 2g
- Fat: 15g
- Carbohydrates: 30g
- Fiber: 2g

Smoothies & Milkshakes: Pureed Banana and Almond Butter Smoothie

Prep Time: 5 minutes

Cooking Time: 0 minutes (No cooking needed)

Total Time: 5 minutes

Serving: 1

Ingredients:

- *1 ripe banana*
- *1 tbsp almond butter*
- *1/2 cup almond milk*
- *1/2 cup ice cubes*
- *1 teaspoon honey (optional)*

Directions:

1. In a blender, mix ripe banana, almond butter, almond milk, ice cubes, and honey (if using).
2. Blend until smooth and creamy.

3. Pour into a glass and drink immediately.

Nutritional Value:

- Calories: 250
- Protein: 4g
- Fat: 12g
- Carbohydrates: 32g
- Fiber: 5g

Berry Blast Smoothie with Greek Yogurt

Prep Time: 5 minutes

Cooking Time: 0 minutes (No cooking needed)

Total Time: 5 minutes

Serving: 1

Ingredients:

- *1/2 cup mixed berries (strawberries, blueberries, raspberries)*
- *1/2 cup Greek yogurt*
- *1/2 cup almond milk*
- *1 tablespoon honey*
- *1/2 cup ice cubes*

Directions:

1. In a blender, add mixed berries, Greek yogurt, almond milk, honey, and ice cubes.

2. Blend until smooth and fully integrated.
3. Pour into a glass and enjoy the berry sweetness.

Nutritional Value:

- o Calories: 180 Protein: 10g
- o Fat: 5g
- o Carbohydrates: 25g
- o Fiber: 4g

Avocado with Mint Chocolate Chip Milkshake

Prep Time: 8 minutes

Cooking Time: 0 minutes (No cooking needed)

Total Time: 8 minutes

Serving: 1

Ingredients:

- o 1 ripe avocado, peeled and pitted
- o 1 cup milk (dairy or plant-based)
- o 2 tbsp chocolate chips
- o 1 tablespoon fresh mint leaves
- o 1 tablespoon honey
- o 1/2 cup ice cubes

Directions:

1. In a blender, add ripe avocado, milk, chocolate chips, fresh mint leaves, honey, and ice cubes.
2. Blend until smooth and chocolaty.
3. Pour into a glass, and experience the minty-chocolate bliss.

Nutritional Value:

- o Calories: 350
- o Protein: 8g
- o Fat: 22g
- o Carbohydrates: 35g
- o Fiber: 8g

Pineapple and Coconut Cream Smoothie

Prep Time: 5 minutes

Cooking Time: 0 minutes (No cooking needed)

Total Time: 5 minutes

Serving: 1

Ingredients:

- o *1 cup fresh pineapple chunks*
- o *1/2 cup coconut milk*
- o *1/2 cup Greek yogurt*
- o *1 tablespoon shredded coconut (optional, for garnish)*
- o *1/2 cup ice cubes*

Directions:

1. In a blender, add fresh pineapple pieces, coconut milk, Greek yogurt, and ice cubes.
2. Blend until smooth and tropical.
3. Pour into a glass, and if desired, garnish with shredded coconut.

Nutritional Value:

- Calories: 220
- Protein: 10g
- Fat: 15g
- Carbohydrates: 18g
- Fiber: 2g

Creamy Fruits & Desserts:

Pureed Peach and Amaretto Cream

Prep Time: 10 minutes

Cooking Time: 0 minutes (No cooking needed)

Total Time: 10 minutes

Serving: 2

Ingredients:

- *2 ripe peaches, pitted and diced*

- o *2 tablespoons amaretto liqueur*
- o *1/4 cup heavy cream*
- o *1 tablespoon honey (optional)*

Directions:

1. Place chopped peaches and amaretto liqueur in a blender or food processor.
2. Puree till smooth.
3. In a second bowl, beat the heavy cream until soft peaks form.
4. Fold the peach puree into the whipped cream until well absorbed.
5. Sweeten with honey if desired.
6. Serve chilled in dessert cups.

Nutritional Value: (per serving)

- o Calories: 180
- o Protein: 2g
- o Fat: 12g
- o Carbohydrates: 18g
- o Fiber: 2g

Creamy Apricot and Almond Puree

Prep Time: 15 minutes

Cooking Time: 0 minutes (No cooking needed)

Total Time: 15 minutes

Serving: 2

Ingredients:

- o *4 ripe apricots, pitted and sliced*
- o *1/4 cup almond butter*
- o *2 tablespoons Greek yogurt*
- o *1 tablespoon honey*

Directions:

1. In a blender, mix cut apricots, almond butter, Greek yogurt, and honey.
2. Blend until smooth and creamy.
3. Adjust sweetness with extra honey if required.
4. Serve chilled in bowls or dessert glasses.

Nutritional Value: (per serving)

- o Calories: 220
- o Protein: 5g
- o Fat: 15g
- o Carbohydrates: 18g
- o Fiber: 4g

Honeyed Fig and Goat Cheese Mousse

Prep Time: 20 minutes

Cooking Time: 0 minutes (No cooking needed)

Total Time: 20 minutes

Serving: 4

Ingredients:

- *8 fresh figs, stems, and half*
- *4 ounces goat cheese*
- *2 tablespoons honey*
- *1/4 cup chopped walnuts (for garnish)*

Directions:

1. In a food processor, combine figs, goat cheese, and honey until smooth.
2. Divide the mixture into serving glasses.
3. Refrigerate for at least 1 hour.
4. Before serving, garnish with chopped walnuts.

Nutritional Value: (per serving)

- Calories: 180
- Protein: 7g
- Fat: 12g
- Carbohydrates: 15g
- Fiber: 3g

Lemon Curd and Blackberry Compote

Prep Time: 15 minutes

Cooking Time: 10 minutes

Total Time: 25 minutes

Serving: 4

Ingredients:

- o *1 cup fresh blackberries*
- o *1/4 cup sugar*
- o *1 tablespoon lemon zest*
- o *2 teaspoons lemon juice*
- o *4 tablespoons lemon curd*

Directions:

1. In a saucepan, mix blackberries, sugar, lemon zest, and lemon juice.
2. Simmer over medium heat until berries break down and the sauce thickens (approximately 10 minutes).
3. Let the blackberry compote cool.
4. In serving glasses, put lemon curd and blackberry compote.
5. Place in the fridge to chill for a minimum of 1 hours before serving.

Nutritional Value: (per serving)

- o Calories: 120
- o Protein: 1g
- o Fat: 3g
- o Carbohydrates: 25g
- o Fiber: 4g

Warm & Comforting Drinks:

Spiced Pumpkin and Cinnamon Hot Chocolate

Prep Time: 5 minutes

Cooking Time: 10 minutes

Total Time: 15 minutes

Serving: 2

Ingredients:

- o *2 cups milk (dairy or plant-based)*
- o *1/2 cup pumpkin puree*
- o *2 teaspoons cocoa powder*
- o *3 tablespoons sugar*
- o *1/2 teaspoon cinnamon*
- o *1/4 teaspoon nutmeg*
- o *1/4 teaspoon vanilla extract*

o   *Whipped cream and cinnamon sticks for garnish (optional)*

Directions:

1. In a saucepan, add milk, pumpkin puree, cocoa powder, sugar, cinnamon, nutmeg, and vanilla essence.
2. Whisk continually over medium heat until heated but not boiling.
3. Pour into cups, then if desired, top with whipped cream and decorate with cinnamon sticks.
4. Serve immediately and enjoy the cozy taste.

Nutritional Value: (per serving)

o   Calories: 180
o   Protein: 7g
o   Fat: 7g
o   Carbohydrates: 25g
o   Fiber: 3g

Pureed Apple and Caramelized Pear Cider

Prep Time: 10 minutes

Cooking Time: 20 minutes

Total Time: 30 minutes

Serving: 4

Ingredients:

- *4 apples, peeled, cored, and diced*
- *2 pears, peeled, cored, and diced*
- *1/4 cup brown sugar*
- *1 teaspoon cinnamon*
- *1/4 teaspoon nutmeg*
- *4 cups water*
- *Caramel sauce for drizzling (optional)*

Directions:

1. In a large saucepan, add apples, pears, brown sugar, cinnamon, nutmeg, and water.
2. Bring to a boil, then decrease heat and simmer for 20 minutes until fruits are tender.
3. Using an immersion blender or blender, puree the ingredients until they are smooth.
4. Strain the purée to eliminate any pulp.
5. Serve warm in cups, then drizzle with caramel sauce if desired.
6. Enjoy the soothing apple and caramelized pear tastes.

Nutritional Value: (per serving)

- Calories: 120
- Protein: 1g
- Fat: 0g
- Carbohydrates: 30g

o Fiber: 5g

Smooth Vanilla and Cardamom-Infused Chai Latte

Prep Time: 5 minutes

Cooking Time: 10 minutes

Total Time: 15 minutes

Serving: 2

Ingredients:

- o *2 cups milk (dairy or plant-based)*
- o *two teaspoons loose black tea leaves or two tea bags*
- o *1/2 teaspoon ground cardamom*
- o *1/2 teaspoon vanilla extract*
- o *2 tablespoons honey or sweetener of choice*
- o *Cinnamon for dusting (optional)*

Directions:

1. In a saucepan, heat milk until it steams (do not boil).
2. Add tea leaves or tea bags, cardamom, vanilla essence, and honey.
3. Steep for 5-7 minutes.
4. Strain the tea into glasses.
5. Optionally, sprinkle with cinnamon before serving.

6. Savor the fragrant vanilla and cardamom overtones in this wonderful chai latte.

Nutritional Value: (per serving)

- o Calories: 120
- o Protein: 6g
- o Fat: 5g
- o Carbohydrates: 15g
- o Fiber: 0g

Festive & Special Occasion Treats:

Raspberry Coulis and Champagne Jelly

Prep Time: 15 minutes

Cooking Time: 10 minutes (for jelly)

Total Time: 4 hours (including cooling time)

Serving: 4

Ingredients:

- o 1 cup raspberries

- 1/4 cup sugar
- 1 cup champagne
- 2 tablespoons gelatin

Directions:

1. In a saucepan, blend raspberries and sugar. Cook over medium heat until raspberries break down.
2. Strain the raspberry mixture to obtain a silky coulis. Set aside.
3. In a separate pot, warm champagne. Sprinkle gelatin over it and let it blossom for a few minutes.
4. Heat the champagne and gelatin mixture until the gelatin dissolves.
5. Pour a layer of raspberry coulis into serving glasses. Let it sit in the refrigerator for 1 hour.
6. Once firm, pour the champagne-gelatin mixture over the coulis layer.
7. Refrigerate for at least 3 hours or until totally set.

Nutritional Value: (per serving)

Calories: 150

Protein: 3g

Fat: 0g

Carbohydrates: 20g

Fiber: 2g

Pistachio with Rosewater Panna Cotta

Prep Time: 15 minutes

Cooking Time: 10 minutes

Total Time: 4 hours (including cooling time)

Serving: 4

Ingredients:

- o *2 cups heavy cream*
- o *1/2 cup sugar*
- o *1/2 cup shelled pistachios*
- o *1 teaspoon rosewater*
- o *2 tablespoons gelatin*

Directions:

1. In a saucepan, simmer heavy cream and sugar until the sugar dissolves.
2. In a blender, purée pistachios with a little cream until smooth.
3. Strain the pistachio puree into the cream mixture.
4. Add rosewater and heat until just before boiling.
5. Sprinkle gelatin over the mixture, whisking continually until totally dissolved.
6. Pour the mixture into molds or serving glasses.

7. Place in the fridge for a minimum of 3 hours or until set before serving.

Nutritional Value: (per serving)

- Calories: 300
- Protein: 5g
- Fat: 25g
- Carbohydrates: 15g
- Fiber: 1g

Pureed Cranberry and Orange Sorbet

Prep Time: 10 minutes

Freezing Time: 4 hours or overnight

Total Time: 4 hours and 10 minutes

Serving: 4

Ingredients:

- *2 cups fresh or frozen cranberries*
- *1/2 cup orange juice*
- *1/2 cup sugar*
- *Zest one orange*

Directions:

1. In a blender, mix cranberries, orange juice, sugar, and orange zest until smooth.

2. Strain the mixture to remove any pulp.
3. Pour the purée into a shallow dish and freeze.
4. Every hour, whisk the liquid with a fork to break up ice crystals.
5. Continue freezing and stirring until the sorbet achieves the desired consistency.

Nutritional Value: (per serving)

- o Calories: 120
- o Protein: 1g
- o Fat: 0g
- o Carbohydrates: 30g
- o Fiber: 3g

Printed in Great Britain
by Amazon

51463344R10071